"Life is a Journey, not a destination." Inspiration, determination, and motivation has been inspired by so many wonderful people encountered on this marvelous adventure we call life. It would be impossible to name everyone responsible for helping me bring this dream to fruition. To Angie, Jenny, Carolyn, Mary Ellen, Mary, Peggy, Charlie, Ann, Melinda, Melissa, my deepest gratitude!

I am most appreciative of the long-lasting love and friendship of L.M. who's been my personal muse throughout many years on this journey.

With deep pain (no pun intended, Dave) and heartfelt gratitude, this book is dedicated to Dave Payne, for his contribution to making this book a reality, for giving me the motivation to move the project "off the back burner and get cooking again," for his ability to balance the seriousness of a sobering subject with his wit and wisdom, and for providing the male perspective that was so invaluable for The Male Teenager's 9 Early Signs of Alcoholism and now The Male Teenager's 9 Middle Signs. Certainly his scenarios were often more insightful from his viewpoint than mine.

Ironically, Dave was in hand-to-hand combat with his own disease the entire time we worked on this project. Unfortunately, he passed away when the first book was moving into editorial review. The last two were about three-quarters finished. Dave wanted to leave a lasting legacy. Hopefully his input into this series will be his greatest contribution, making a difference in a world that still doesn't understand how baffling, cunning, powerful, and insidious this disease truly is. He believed that young people need to recognize these early signs and become familiar with the available resources in order to get help earlier for this misunderstood malady.

Dave, thank you for your help. Your suggestions will continue to guide and motivate me to complete the series in your memory.

THE MALE TEENAGER'S

NINE MIDDLE SIGNS
OF ALCOHOLISM

Becki Bateman, with Dave Payne

InspiringVoices®
A Service of **Guideposts**

Inspiring Voices books may be ordered through booksellers or by contacting:

Inspiring Voices
1663 Liberty Drive
Bloomington, IN 47403
www.inspiringvoices.com
1-(866) 697-5313

Because of the dynamic nature of the Internet, any web addresses or links contained in this book may have changed since publication and may no longer be valid. The views expressed in this work are solely those of the author and do not necessarily reflect the views of the publisher, and the publisher hereby disclaims any responsibility for them.

Any people depicted in stock imagery provided by Thinkstock are models, and such images are being used for illustrative purposes only.

Certain stock imagery © Thinkstock.

ISBN: 978-1-4624-0591-6 (sc)
ISBN: 978-1-4624-0592-3 (e)

Library of Congress Control Number: 2013906685

Printed in the United States of America.

Inspiring Voices rev. date: 04/18/13

By the same author

ALERT (Actual Learning Examples to
Recognize Trouble) Series:

The Male Teenager's 9 Early Signs of Alcoholism
The Male Teenager's 9 Middle Signs of Alcoholism
The Male Teenager's 9 Late Signs of Alcoholism

Future publications:
The Female Teenager's 9 Early Signs of Alcoholism
The Female Teenager's 9 Middle Signs of Alcoholism
The Female Teenager's 9 Late Signs of Alcoholism

HINTS (Helpful Information Needed To Succeed) Series

CONGRATULATIONS! YOU HAVE CHOSEN THE second book in the CALERT (Actual Learning Examples of Recognizing Trouble) series. After reading this book, *The Male Teenager's 9 Middle Signs of Alcoholism*, you should have a better idea how to recognize a young man's behavior that might indicate these middle signals after his disease progresses through early-stage alcoholism into this second stage. Let us begin with some background information.

As you are reading, keep in mind that this series is not intended to be a collection of statistics or rendering of research. With 232 million sites on the Internet alone and thousands of books at local libraries and bookshops, we suggest you gather information as it relates to and interest you. At the end of each book in the series, there are listed resources and Web sites where you can gather pertinent information relevant to your personal journey.

In the 80's, when the subject of alcoholism became popular on TV talk shows, in the movies, and in books on alcoholism, co-dependency, and adult children of alcoholics there was an explosion of knowledge; many of the books made it to the best seller lists. At the same time there were national conferences such as the Annual Conference on Alcoholism and the Family and Adult Children of Alcoholics that drew focus to this problem. Unfortunately, over the next 30 years the hoopla has died down, but the problem has not. A vast amount of people still carry a stereotype of what a "typical" alcoholic looks and acts like.

If you are asked to close your eyes and picture an alcoholic, do you picture an old person on a street corner panhandling for money, a homeless person sleeping under a bridge or a piece of cardboard, or someone who is eating out of a dumpster? When you picture alcoholics, were any of them young? Were they all male? Such images would not be entirely wrong; however, you would be picturing alcoholics in chronic or late-stage alcoholism, which is only 3 percent of the alcoholic population. No one wakes up in the chronic-stage alcoholism; each and every drinker has had to go through the early and middle stages first.

Statistically, it is roughly 50 percent male and 50 percent female who are alcoholics. Younger and younger people are being treated for this affliction. Alcoholism doesn't discriminate. It will take any age, color, ethnic group, or occupation into its grip. For example, did you envision alcoholic professionals such as doctors, nurses, teachers, lawyers, or clergymen? Name any occupation, and ten percent are alcoholics in one of the three stages. They are referred to as "functioning" alcoholics.

"FUNCTIONING" ALCOHOLICS ARE PEOPLE WHO do not show any clear signs of having a problem. They perform while on-the-job, are rarely absent, and often are cited for their exemplary work. Some specific examples of those working in the helping professions and in one of the three stages of alcoholism themselves are:

- A professor who comes to work every day, and is a "weekend warrior" – that is she drinks heavily on weekends consuming as much then as someone else might throughout the week

- A lawyer whose caseload is 79 percent alcohol related and works to help these people; yet he "nips" alcohol throughout his day

- A social worker who does not realize the majority of her caseloads are alcohol and/or drug-related. She works to help them with their problems, yet she keeps her wine glass filled once she leaves work

- A counselor who helps scores of young men and women with their problems dealing with alcohol, but he has alcohol hidden in drawers or bookshelves at work

- A surgeon, doctor, or nurse who treats and/or operates on sick alcoholics, but she does not recognize her affliction with alcoholism because she is in the middle stage and does not realize it

- A pilot who navigates a plane while under the influence, but he does not see this as a problem with alcohol.

The list could go on and on as 10 percent of people in any given occupation are alcoholics. Family, friends, and clients have absolutely no idea of these professionals dependence on alcohol.

ONE OF THE MOST PROFOUND quotes from his movie, "Chalk Talk on Alcoholism", was from Father Joseph Martin, well-known in the field of alcoholism. He stated, "By the time an alcoholic is in chronic stage alcoholism any moron would know he's got a problem. That is only three percent of the alcoholic population. We, as a society, need to be more informed about the other 97 percent that are not in chronic alcoholism, but have the potential to be." He also stated, "If alcohol causes a problem, then it *is* a problem."

Many people in the 97 percent could be teenagers, yet this age group has not been adequately identified or addressed. Teens in general have a tougher time identifying with alcoholism. They can give many reasons why they're *not* alcoholics. They are too young; they have not usually experienced the loss of jobs, families, homes, or material things; they haven't been kicked out of school, or served time in jail or prison. They only party on the weekends "like everyone else" or they "only have a couple" once in awhile. Teens do not recognize the early signs of alcoholism, let alone the middle signs.

If teens have not had a job to lose, have not started their own families, or acquired a significant amount of material things they will not have some of the losses that can indicate earlier problems with drinking. Most teens are not apt to do anything illegal or create problems to warrant getting arrested. If they encounter legal issues they usually still rely on their parents. Mom and Dad will sometimes deny that their kids have a problem. They may actually defend their son or daughter and/or bail him or her out of jail so the child doesn't suffer any consequences for the behavior.

There are nine signs in each of the three stages of alcoholism (early, middle, and late). This is a total of 27 indicators. How many teens would recognize them? More importantly, would they be able to cite specific examples in their own drinking patterns that relate to these signs?

In reality, each person is different, so the examples presented in this book and the other two in the series could not possibly indicate all the ways and means a young person initially shows the symptoms of this disease. Yes, in the early '50's the American Medical Association deemed alcoholism a disease. The reasons it was classified as a disease are:

1. There are four identifiable groups of people prone to this disease in our society – Children of Alcoholics, Native Americans, Teetotlers, and minority groups.
2. There are three stages - early, middle, and late - each with nine symptoms.
3. Alcoholism is progressive and it gets worse in each stage.
4. There is no cure for this malady, but it can be arrested by not taking the first drink!

EACH OF THE NINE MIDDLE-STAGE signs will be presented with three or more possible scenarios. We have already met J.D. in the first book, *The Male Teenager's 9 Early Signs of Alcoholism*, as he progressed through the first stage. The examples in this book offer a variety of situations that will show how J.D. is exhibiting the middle stage symptoms. If you think you may have a drinking problem try to identify with each scenario as you read this. Look for ways you are like J.D., not how you are different from him. Or, if you are reading this because you are concerned about a friend or relative who may be experiencing problems with alcohol, try to think of this person and how he or she would exhibit each one of the middle signs and how you might be of help.

Keep in mind that every teen will progress at a different rate. He could remain in the early stage for ten to twenty years or for as little as a year or less. Many variables (e.g. the age he began drinking, his body chemistry, his height and weight, the amount he drinks, how often he drinks, what he drinks, what, if any, substances that he ingests into his body while drinking, etc) can affect the length of time in any stage.

It is not unusual for a teen to have started drinking before the age of thirteen. The younger a person is when he picks up the drink, the faster it affects him; his body, bones, and organs are still forming. A teen who weighs 95 pounds will progress through the stages faster than a young person weighing 140 lbs. or more. The five- foot-six-inch teen will also progress faster than the teen over six feet tall. A younger child drinking daily will show signs more quickly than a teen drinking a couple bottles of wine three or four times a week. If any other substances (drugs and/or pills, for example) are used while the young man is drinking, he will rapidly progress. Considering such factors, it is possible to go through the early stages of alcoholism in five years or less. If he begins using alcohol at thirteen he might enter the middle stage around eighteen, and he could be in the late stages of addiction in his early twenties! Again, each person's inner chemical makeup reacts differently to the alcohol and/or the substances he takes into his body. This also explains why we are seeing younger and younger kids ending up in hospitals, detox, rehabilitation centers, and other institutions.

If each stage takes a longer time then the person could be considerably older or in the final stage. This also explains why one might think of an alcoholic as someone older.

N O ONE WAKES UP ONE morning and finds himself in late stage alcoholism. He has to progress through each of the three stages - early, middle, and late.

Here's a quick overview of each stage and its symptoms as identified by the American Medical Association:

The nine EARLY signs:

1. Hide it
2. Sneak/steal it
3. Angry when someone tries to talk to you about your drinking
4. Blame other people/places/things
5. Drink when something bad/good happens
6. Drink until supply is gone
7. Change in personality
8. Uncomfortable when not available
9. Blackouts

The nine MIDDLE signs:

1. Drink before a function
2. Loss of other interests
3. Preoccupation with drinking
4. Promises and Resolutions fail repeatedly
5. Neglect personal care: hygiene/food/health
6. Problems with family, friends, work, school, money, etc.
7. Increased tolerance
8. Increased dependence
9. Blackouts – more frequent, longer in duration

The nine LATE signs:

1. Loss of family, friends, jobs
2. Loss of willpower (self-control)
3. Obsession with alcohol
4. Physical and moral deterioration
5. Decreased intolerance
6. Drinking with inferiors or alone
7. Impaired thinking
8. Geographical cures
9. Mental health facilities/hospitals, jails, or DEATH

NOW LET US REVIEW THE first book in the series of *The Male Teenager's 9 Early Signs of Alcoholism*. J.D. was in his early teenage years. He seemed to be a typical teen with an older brother and younger sister. His dad was a lab technician and his mom a social worker. They looked like the all-American family, but J.D. never felt like he fit in. When he first began drinking he hid the booze in soda cans and bottles; he never thought of hiding milk or soda in other containers. He would hide alcohol in numerous spots around the house; the thought of hiding cocoa or lemonade in the attic, cellar, or storage areas never crossed his mind. Outside the house he would bury his liquor bottles at the bottom of boxes marked "scrapbooks" that were stored in the shed; in his entire life he had never consciously put any other kind of bottle or can in a box marked so differently. If someone would walk into a room and surprise him when he was drinking, J.D. would immediately conceal it behind a chair or a curtain; he never hid any kind of nonalcoholic drink.

How would J.D. sneak or steal alcohol? He knew where the key to his parent's liquor cabinet was kept and would pour out some from the bottle and replace it with water so they would not discover any was missing; he never stole soda or watered any of that down to hide the theft. J.D. would conceal a six pack under his jacket and sneak that into the house; there was no time J.D. had purchased milk or soda that he would do that. J.D. took more for his supply from an uncle who had a bar in his basement. He also stole money from his parents and grandparents to purchase alcohol and he would talk friends into buying it for him; he had never done this sort of theft for nonalcoholic beverages. Another risky thing he did was breaking into a house taking only beer and liquor; he had never robbed any home of milk or soda. J.D. also had a friend working at a local convenience store. He had used friends to get them to buy beer or help him steal some wine from the store, not caring if his friends would get in trouble or lose their jobs; he only stole alcohol. At no point in his life had he ever used his friendships to get anyone to buy him kool-aid or soda or put their job in jeopardy for him.

J.D. would also get angry when different people tried to talk to him about his drinking and the changes in his behavior. He not only broke up with a girlfriend when she attempted to talk to him about her concerns with his drinking, but also he alienated other friends with his attitude when they would try to point out that maybe he was drinking too much. J.D.'s parents got the brunt of his anger when they tried to discuss his drinking. Some teachers and his principle also noticed his grades had dropped and that he had skipped several classes. When they attempted to get him to discuss these concerns, again he just got angry. J.D. did not react this way when people tried to talk to him about other matters unrelated to drinking.

J.D. was adept at blaming other people, places, and things with incidences related to drinking. If he drank too much, then someone else had spiked the drink. Or if he got so loaded and missed curfew, he would blame it on his friends. J.D. would place the blame back on his family when they questioned him as to why he never attended family get-togethers anymore. He would blame the bosses when he lost his part-time jobs at age fifteen and sixteen. Other excuses for his poor attitude and behaviors were the customers who agitated him, school, and the teachers whom he believed were pointing fingers at him. He used these as additional excuses for why he felt the need to drink. When he thought people were talking about him, a couple drinks could also calm him down.

It did not take much for J.D. to drink when something bad would happen or when something good happened. The death of his grandfather, his unexpected cut from the football team, and trouble with the law were just a few of the low points which gave him an excuse to drink. On the other hand getting out of school for a vacation, acing a test when he thought he had failed it, his baseball team winning a regional championship, and getting a totally unexpected award at a school assembly were good enough reasons for him to drink to celebrate these happier moments.

J.D. COULD NOT STAND TO see booze go to waste. If others did not drink it, he would. If his friends left any beer, he would finish it off even though he had probably passed the legal limit. He would see glasses of liquor left at a family gathering and go around gulping down the remainder. Often he and his buddies would have friendly poker games and whenever he spotted cans that were left on the table, he would check for leftover liquor. If so, he would drink it; no sense in wasting any!

J.D. never felt like he fit in anywhere. Yet as soon as he would begin to drink, "Mr. Misfit" would become "Mr. Entertainer". Other times he might say things just to instigate a fight. Sometimes these arguments would lead to a confrontation. The scary thing was he did not seem to care about the size of the other guy; he was ready to take on anybody. He was very shy with the girls, but once he had a couple drinks in him he thought he was "Mr. Charmer". These are just some of the ways in which his personality changed after he started drinking.

Places J.D. went were selected by knowing ahead of time that alcohol would be available and that his age would not be questioned. He felt if he could not drink his chance of having a good time was nil. If he knew alcohol would not be served he would hide his own supply. He found himself drifting away from all his old friends and hanging out with guys who were older and liked to party.

J.D. had no idea that blackouts were also an early indicator of alcoholism. He thought everyone who drank experienced them; he also confused blacking out with passing out. A blackout means a person can function but will not remember what he has done or only recall parts of it when he sobers up. Passing out is getting so drunk that a person's brain and body literally shut down... on a bed, a friend's couch, a front lawn, the street, etc. J.D. is having more blackouts. His friends are telling him things he says or does while he is drinking; yet he has absolutely no recollection of these experiences.

Now that you have an idea of how J.D.'s alcoholism is progressing let's get acquainted with how his disease demonstrates signs for the middle stage symptoms.

1. Drink Before A Function

J.D. DID NOT NOTICE THAT gradually he needs some "liquid courage" to go to school functions or carry out some kind of class assignment. He finds that if he takes a few drinks before a school dance, he has a much better time. Previously when he walked into a dance he would be very uncomfortable and could not be sociable. He was especially tongue-tied with the girls, and would stand off in a corner being miserable while everyone else seemed to be having a terrific time. He quickly learned that when he drinks his tongue loosens up and so do his feet. He is Robert Pattinson, the heartthrob magnet with the girls, and Fred Astaire on the dance floor. He even keeps a bottle hidden outside so if the buzz is wearing off he can recapture it. Alcohol helps him give a captivating talk when assigned one in speech class. He also convinces himself he is more relaxed to take exams when he drinks before them.

He believes he plays sports with more skill if he drinks before the challenge. J.D. plays in every football game of the season. He and his friends always celebrate with a couple of drinks after the game. This year, with the team in the state finals, a group of his friends are planning to go. He knows he will need to drink with them on the way there. With a few drinks in him he can be so much more vocally supportive to his team.

J.D. definitely has a more enjoyable time at a concert when he is under the influence. He and his friends have concert tickets to a rock group that is making a tour stop in his town. The big night is right around the corner. As the time draws nearer he worries whether he will be in the right frame of mind to enjoy it. In the past he has gone to concerts sober and noticed his friends seem to enjoy themselves a lot more than he did because they were drinking. So he decides to have a few drinks before concerts and to also take a flask so he can keep the buzz throughout the evening.

He believes he is a regular card whiz when the guys get together for their weekly poker games if he has something to drink before they begin. Each time he drinks before any kind of function, it reinforces how much he relies on his "best friend" to put him at ease.

These examples show how J.D. is beginning to move into middle stage alcoholism. Now, can you come up with a few other examples of when teenage boys think they need some "liquid courage" to go to some type of social event?

2. Loss Of Other Interests

J.D. AND HIS OLD FRIENDS spent a lot of time hanging out and listening to music. Gradually he makes hundreds of excuses why he does not have time for them anymore. He is now spending a great deal of time with his new friends. These guys like to drink, party, and have real fun!

Previously he liked to listen to music. He took guitar lessons for over six months because his parents had bought him the guitar and paid for all the lessons. Now without discussing it with them he decides to quit taking lessons. His argument is that he had way too much homework and his part-time job was a killer; there just is not enough extra time for these lessons. He prefers to use this time with his new friends because they understand him!

J.D.'s parents have also spent a bundle of money on art supplies and a year of lessons to nurture a talent he exhibited at a very early age. Now, without saying a word to them, he quits going to the lessons. After missing several weeks of instruction, the teacher calls his parents. They are not at all pleased to learn in this way that their son has wasted another opportunity on which they have spent so much of their hard- earned money. Of course, an argument ensues and J.D. has another excuse to hit the bottle.

J.D. joins several after-school clubs. He is active in the Barnstormers, a theater group, and enjoys helping with props and painting the scenery. In addition, he is volunteering at a local hospital helping to serve some of the patients at mealtime. Soon he is making excuses and not keeping his commitment to either of these activities. He figures they won't miss him and that they have plenty of other help.

Another past time for J.D. is playing Xbox with his friends after school. They get together and occasionally have a couple beers. As time goes on he desires alcohol more than playing the video games. Drinking becomes the main focus of these get-togethers after school. By now he is slowly drifting away from all his buddies from elementary and middle school. He hangs out with this older group who like to do the same things that he does –drink and party!

These are some of the interests that a teen often has and gradually replaces with drinking and more drinking. How many more examples of this middle sign of alcoholism have you experienced or observed in others?

3. Preoccupation With Drinking

J.D. USED TO ENJOY SCHOOL and his classes. Constantly thinking of alcohol interferes with his performance at school in different ways. He is so completely absorbed in these thoughts that when the teacher calls on him he either does not hear the question or picks up a keyword or two and tries to respond. When he gets caught not paying attention, the other kids in the class laugh and he is embarrassed. This is affecting his overall performance in his classes. With his thoughts concentrated on drinking activities, he is not able to focus in or out of class on his schoolwork; he may be physically in the classroom, but his mind is somewhere else. His homework is suffering. He does not do all of his homework, and if he does complete an assignment it will be late. He is failing more and more

of his tests. Lately he finds himself preoccupied with the clock and waiting for the bell to ring. All he has on his mind is when and where he and his friends will go, what they will have to drink, and who else might be there. The time just seems to drag on and on. J.D. doesn't have a clue how much valuable time booze is stealing from him. At seventeen he is seriously considering quitting school.

The weekend is coming and he is invited to a party. All week the majority of J.D.'s thoughts have been about what he was going to tell his parents in order to get out of the house. He knows they will never allow him to go to a party where everyone will be drinking. He is also spending a great deal of time plotting and planning how he can get some money so he can contribute his fair share of the booze. He certainly does not want his parents to learn that his friend's parents will allow underage kids to drink at the party.

When J.D. is engaged in conversation his mind often drifts off to alcohol. He then asks them to repeat something or nods his head in agreement as though he is paying attention. He is especially doing this more and more with his own family.

What other examples of teens being preoccupied with drinking can you think of for this middle-stage warning sign?

4. Promises And Resolutions Fail Repeatedly

J.D. BREAKS PROMISES TO HIS older brother and younger sister more and more frequently. In one week alone he tells his brother he will go to the baseball game with him, but backs out at the last minute. He makes a date with his little sister to go to her dance recital that she has been begging him to attend, but he forgets about it. He makes excuses for not helping his father fix his sister's bicycle as he promised. Each time he has received a call from his friends and decides he will have a much better time with them at a party.

After partying on a Tuesday night J.D. goes to school with a terrible hangover. He promises himself that he will never drink on a school night again. That promise lasted for about a week. The following Thursday a couple of friends invite him to their house. Friday brings another terrible hangover.

J.D. makes hundreds of resolutions. Maybe you have made some yourself:

I will help my folks around the house more.
I will keep my bedroom neater.
I will respect my curfew and get in on time.
I will call up a couple long-lost cousins and check on them.
I will have a better attitude with my teachers.
I will hand in all my assignments on time.
I will answer more questions in class.

I will study more so I can do better on my tests.

I will pay better attention in class.

I will be kinder to my younger sister.

I will ask my older brother to help me in math.

I will call up some of my old buddies and
    see what they are doing.

I will not cut classes anymore.

I will not agitate my brother so much.

I will not drink so much next time.

I will not be so obnoxious to my friends anymore.

I will not go to places anymore that serve underage kids.

I will not hang around the rough crowd anymore.

I will not drink hard liquor anymore.

I will not spend so much money on booze.

I will not allow anyone to get my goat.

I will not call *that* person anymore.

I will not hang out in *that* place anymore.

I will not do *that* anymore. (whatever *that* is)

The same thing happens again and again with more frequency. Of course he tells himself each time this will be the *last* time!

Can you think of some other promises or resolutions a teen could make and continually fail to keep?

5. Personal Care: Hygiene, Food, Health

ONE DAY WHILE SITTING IN the cafeteria a friend of J.D.'s tells him about a party coming up on the weekend. J.D. has already blown his allowance. He knows in order to have money to buy booze for the party he will have to go without lunch the rest of the week. He will sneak a sandwich or two out of the house and his parents will not be the wiser.

J.D. finds he is not as hungry as he used to be. He is also not eating his mother's healthy meals much at home anymore, but grabbing junk food that he can eat on the fly. The junk food does not seem to taste as good and also fills him up so he cannot drink as much. He gradually cuts down on the amount of food he is eating so he can leave room for more drinking. Also if he does not eat as much he is getting a better buzz.

After a really heavy night of drinking, J.D. awakens 30 minutes past his normal time. He realizes he has fallen asleep wearing the same clothes from the night before. In order to get to school on time he skips his shower and wears what he has on even though the outfit is wrinkled, stained, and smelly.

J.D.'s hair looks like it could use a cut and a good shampooing. He always prided himself on his appearance but now is looking grubbier and grubbier. A lot of the time his clothes are in need of mending, ironing, and/or washing. Lately it does not seem to matter to him.

Each year J.D. usually goes for an eye check up, a dental visit, and an annual physical. This year he cancels each one with excuses, because he has "more important" things to do. In addition he has always been very concerned with staying fit. He has a very strenuous workout. More and more frequently he is shortening it or skipping it altogether.

In the past he ridiculed people who smoked and reeked of it. Now when he is drinking he will often light up a cigarette to impress his new friends. Sure he has heard the commercials that explain the health consequences from smoking, but the need to impress his friends is more important to him at this point.

These are a few examples of how a teenager might neglect himself in the areas of hygiene, food, and health. Can you cite some other examples to illustrate these middle signs?

6. Problems: Family, School, Work, And Money

FAMILY

J.D.'s PARENTS ARE CONCERNED THAT he seldom joins in family activities, spends too much time alone in his room, ignores church attendance, and seldom does things with his old friends from elementary school. Excuses and lies are becoming more common. At times J.D. himself has trouble distinguishing truth from fiction. His parents have actually threatened to get him help for his problem! "What problem?" he fumes to himself.

Finally J.D.'s parents are fed up. They try to tell him he is becoming a bad influence on his brother and sister and they think he is slowly destroying himself. He is not holding up his end of responsibility within the family. He neglects doing chores around the house. He is not keeping his own room clean. His disrespect for them in front of his siblings is not acceptable behavior. His parents make arrangements for him to go live with an uncle. There he will not have to change schools and can finish up his senior year. J.D. rebels against this idea! As a legal eighteen-year-old adult he refuses to live in his uncle's home, and instead moves in with one of his buddies. He is sure this guy will let him crash on his couch in his one-bedroom apartment.

School

In his earlier school days J.D. was on the honor roll several times. But over the years his grades steadily declined. Some of his teachers continued to warn him that if his grades did not improve he would fail their course and endanger the entire school year. His coaches also threatened to kick him off the baseball and football teams because he would be academically ineligible if he did not straighten up his act. J.D. forgot to do homework assignments or handed them in late if he did complete them. More and more he was skipping classes. He wondered why everyone was on his case!

Work

When J.D. turned seventeen he got his third part-time job, having been fired from the first two. In this job he pumped gas at one of the last full-service stations in his town. This job lasted longer, but he was still fired because of his old behaviors of tardiness, calling in sick too many times, and being a no-show. Several weeks later he found employment as a part-time mechanic. It did not take him long to decide he was not cut out to be a grease monkey, so he quit. Next J.D. found a part-time job in a restaurant. Within days he was called into the office by the boss who spoke to him about his appearance for the third time. He was told that if he did not take the suggestions seriously he would be fired. "Three strikes and you're out," the boss said as he fired him a few days later. J.D. was lucky to get job number six as a clerk in a local discount store, but within two weeks he lost that due to his tardiness and absenteeism. It took a month before he landed another job. This one was on a construction site delivering necessary supplies for the crews. Too many mistakes cost him this job! In the next few months he clerked in a sporting goods store, washed dishes at a diner, made sandwiches in a deli, and stocked shelves at a warehouse. It is not surprising that his attitude and behaviors got him fired from all these jobs. He could not believe his luck when he got his first full-time job working nights unloading trucks. This was just a very short stint and once again he was quickly fired. He was not even out of his teens yet had been hired and fired a dozen times!

Money

On a daily basis J.D. kept borrowing more and more spending money. He had trouble finding legitimate excuses as to why he was always short of cash. He worried that the people from whom he borrowed money would discover that he used it to buy beer and liquor. People questioned him about what he did with the money he earned when he was working.

How many other problems can a teen have with family, work, school, and money during this middle-stage symptom?

7. Increased Tolerance

WHEN J.D. FIRST STARTED DRINKING 3 or 4 beers gave him a nice buzz. Gradually, it now takes the whole six- pack to give him the same effect. Soon after that he has to drink several more beers to achieve the same initial high.

Although J.D. drinks a lot more he does not show any of the obvious signs of intoxication. He does not slur his words, stumble or stagger while walking, nor get loud and obnoxious. He prides himself that he shows none of the obvious signs of intoxication.

He does, however, think he is sober enough to go to his new job and that no one will suspect he has had "just a couple." In the matter of a few hours he drops a carton filled with bottles of juice, cuts his hand on some of the broken glass, rams his head on a cupboard door he leaves open, and believes no one notices anything unusual about his behavior.

He can drink a lot before he shows any signs of being drunk; he prides himself when he brags he can drink with the best of them. He thinks some of these older guys cannot hold their liquor and do not know how to party. He begins to party earlier in the evening and lasts into the wee hours of the next morning. "What is wrong with those guys? They must be amateurs. I can drink these guys under the table," he says to himself.

Can you name other ways that indicate a teenager can be experiencing increased tolerance to alcohol?

8. Increased Dependence

J.D. denies to himself that he is drinking in the morning, but he finds that after a night of heavy drinking a couple quick drinks in the morning straighten him out so he can function "normally". Now he is not afraid to get wasted because he believes he has found the "magical miracle quick cure".

After taking one of these quick cures he faces a math test and is amazed that he passed it. He now has no fear of taking tests after a night of partying; his hangovers and academic woes are no longer a problem since he knows the solution.

He cannot go anywhere that he is not thinking about who is going to be there, whether there will be a variety of things to drink, what he will need to bring, whether he will have to hide some alcohol so he has a little stash in case the party runs out, whether there will be cute girls who really like to party, and the questions continually run around in his head.

J.D. realizes his whole social life is so much more fun when he is drinking "just a couple" to take the edge off. He tells jokes better, gets girls up on the dance floor, and dances like a pro. He even shocks himself when he gets up on Open Mike Night and sings! He gets dubbed "Mr. Entertainer" and basks at this new attention. He has never been so popular.

J.D. begins to hate going to work. His boss is continually finding fault about what J.D. forgets to do, could have done better, or his overall lack of cooperation and poor quality of work. Coworkers are complaining to the boss about him; they and the boss are driving him nuts. He knows if he has a couple drinks before and during work he can tolerate these guys.

More and more J.D. needs liquid courage so he can face people in his life, gear up for the places he goes, and manage all the things he has to do. For example, he drinks before he goes to talk to a teacher. He has been told his boss wants him to take some supplies to a department upstairs; it is rumored the guy up there is rude and crude. A little nip will help J.D. go up there and face him. Lately J.D.'s way of managing things is to ignore others and "crawl into a bottle". By doing that he believes he does not have to think of those "things" at all now.

Can you name other ways teenagers experience increased dependence upon alcohol to make them feel better or function better?

9. Blackouts
More Frequent, Longer In Duration

NOT ALL DRINKERS EXPERIENCE THIS last middle-stage warning sign of alcoholism, but if one does then it could be a major indicator: it is called a blackout. Most teens confuse blacking out with passing out. Passing out means a person drinks to the point where he becomes unconscious. He may pass out on his bed, on the kitchen floor, a neighbor's patio, in the gutter, etc. In a blackout the person is functioning normally. Later on when the teen tries to recall certain people, places, things, and actions he cannot remember them.

At first J.D. only experienced a couple blackouts in a six month period, and he could recall most of what happened while he had been drinking. But lately he is having a blackout every other week with greater gaps of memory loss. If his friends had not mentioned some things he had done while drinking, he never would have known! This is the beginning of his blackouts becoming more frequent and longer in duration. Below are experiences that caused J.D. more anxiety.

J.D. went to a friend's house and they ended up crashing a party. He was partially drunk when he arrived and proceeded to drink even more so he could "really tie on a good one". The next thing he remembered was awakening in a strange place, but had no idea how he had gotten there. He stumbled out of the empty house and asked someone on the street where he was. How did he get on the other side of town?

The following weekend the same thing happened. He went to a friend's house, began drinking, and they sneaked to an uninvited gathering. The next morning he woke up and again did not recognize his surroundings. As he looked around trying to get his bearings, he spotted some liquor bottles on a shelf. What luck! Immediately he began drinking again. Later the sunshine awakened him on a couch in still another unfamiliar place. From a guy there he learned it was now Sunday morning. Where did Saturday go? The guy gave him a ride home. From home he called his friends and they assured him he was the life of the party that weekend!

Frequently J.D. got home and went to bed, but did not remember how or when he managed that. This was becoming a regular occurrence. He kept telling himself that he would never get so wasted again, yet it kept happening time after time.

There were occasions when he awakened from a blackout wearing another outfit and had no idea when he changed or where he got the clothes. This clothing was nothing he would choose to wear.

Often there can be severe consequences for things one does not even remember while under the influence of alcohol. How long will it be before J.D. does something while under the influence that really causes him even greater problems?

Can you think of some other possibilities for this last warning sign of the middle stage?

MANY YOUNG PEOPLE FAIL TO recognize these middle signs of alcoholism, but once you are aware of what to look for, you can see a potential problem and get help early. If you recognize two or more of these symptoms in one of your friends or even yourself as you read about J. D., ask for help. Remember, alcoholism is the only disease known to man that the longer you have this addiction, the more it convinces you that you don't!

Now that you are more aware of the middle signs of alcoholism, you may want to check out the other two books in this series, *The Male Teenager's 9 Early Signs of Alcoholism* or, *The Male Teenager's 9 Late Signs of Alcoholism.*

Father Joseph Martin said, "If you had a friend or relative with cancer or other serious disease, wouldn't you get your hands on everything you could read to help them? I suggest you do the same thing with the disease of alcoholism." With that quote in mind, here are a few resources you can go to for further information:

Check the Yellow Pages for *Alcoholics Anonymous, alcoholism, treatment centers, Reach Out, rehabilitation services,* or, in the government offices section, found in the front section of many phone books, see the listing under "county" for *alcohol substance abuse services* or *chemical dependency services* or the listing under "state" for the health care hotline. Your local hospitals can also provide more information.

If you have never attended a self-help meeting or group, try to go to at least a dozen meetings to get a feel for which group you can best relate. Unfortunately, many people have preconceived notions about these groups that are not always true. Go to a meeting telling yourself you will learn at least one thing; if you identify with anyone or with any topic discussed, consider attending that group again. If you think you did not learn anything, go to another meeting in your area. Try not to convince yourself that some of the suggestions will not work before you try any. There are over a hundred self-help groups that can further your understanding. The following are some of the most widely known for alcoholism:

Alanon - The only requirement for membership is that there is a problem with alcoholism in a relative or friend.

Alateen - a fellowship for teenagers that the only requirement for membership is that there is a problem with alcoholism in a relative or friend.

Alcoholics Anonymous - The only requirement for membership is a desire to stop drinking.

Children of Alcoholics or Adult Children of Alcoholics – These two programs are for men and women who grew up in alcoholic or other dysfunctional homes.

Co-Dependents Anonymous – The only requirement for membership is a desire for healthy and loving relationships.

Families Anonymous – This is a program for families and friends who have known a feeling of desperation concerning the destructive behavior of someone very near to them whether caused by drugs, alcohol, or other related behaviors.

NUMEROUS PROMINENT PEOPLE HAVE MADE significant contributions in the field of alcoholism and addiction. An Internet search and a review of their Wikipedia pages will help you find valuable information. The following people living or deceased have left a lasting legacy in the field of writing, teaching, training, speaking, or conducting workshops and seminars:

Melody Beattie - best known for her books *Codependent No More: How to Stop Controlling Others, Beyond Codependency and Getting Better All the Time, The Language of Letting Go, and Start Caring for Yourself* (www.melodybeattie.com)

Claudia Black - best known for her book *"It Will Never Happen to Me" Children of Alcoholics: As Youngsters -Adolescents - Adults* (www.claudiablack.com)

John Bradshaw - hosted numerous programs on PBS based on his books (www.johnbradshaw.com)

Betty Ford - the outspoken First Lady who founded Betty Ford Treatment Center

Ernie Larsen -best known for his Stage II Recovery process

John Lee - best known for his book *The Flying Boy: Healing the Wounded Man* (www.johnleebooks.com)

Marty Mann - the "First Lady of Alcoholics Anonymous," who went on to found the National Council on Alcoholism

Father Joseph Martin - a Roman Catholic priest, recovered alcoholic, and renowned speaker known for his video, *Chalk Talk on Alcoholism* and numerous other videos and publications.

M. Scott Peck - the author of *The Road Less Traveled* and fourteen other books

Dr. Robert Smith - cofounder of Alcoholics Anonymous

Robert Subby - best known for his book *Lost in the Shuffle*

Sharon Wegscheider-Cruse - best known for her book *Another Chance: Hope and Health for the Alcoholic Family*

(www.sharonwcruse.com

Bill Wilson - cofounder of Alcoholics Anonymous

Janet Woititz - know for her extensive work concerning adult children of alcoholics

Miscellaneous resources:

National Institute on Alcohol Abuse and Alcoholism 5635 Fisher Lane MSC 9304 Bethesda, MD 20892-9304 1-301-443-3860 www.niaaa.nih.gov/

www.nlm.nih.gov/medlineplus

I F YOU DO AN INTERNET search for "films about alcohol and alcoholism," you will be given the names of some classic ones, such as *The Lost Weekend, Days of Wine and Roses,* and *Leaving Las Vegas.* Other films worth looking into include *My Name is Bill W.,* the story of Alcoholics Anonymous cofounder Bill Wilson, and *When Love Is Not Enough,* the story of Lois Wilson, founder of Alanon and wife of Bill Wilson.

There are over 232,000,000 Web sites that result from a search just on "statistics for alcoholism," so you can see why it would be impossible to list them all. Here are some search terms to get you started:

Alcohol abuse

Current statistics on alcoholism

Adult alcohol abuse

Alcoholism

National statistics on alcoholism

Alcohol statistics by race

Alcohol-related deaths

Alcoholism family statistics

Statistics on alcohol in America

Alcohol consumption

Alcohol parent statistics

Of course, libraries are an excellent resource, as they have books, cassettes, magazines, books on tape, CDs, and DVDs on alcohol and alcoholism.

It is our sincere hope that this list of resources will enhance your journey to sobriety.

ABOUT THE AUTHOR

B ECKI BATEMAN EARNED A BS and an MA in education in the 60's and early 70's. It was at the beginning of 1978 that she began her own personal recovery journey. The only reason she went to a self-help meeting was to find answers to get those people causing chaos, calamities, and crisis in her life to straighten up so she would be okay! While attending those meetings she got to see videos, read books, and hear material on the family disease of alcoholism. She recognized herself when they talked about the "hero" or "super responsible" one in the family. She was like a sponge soaking up this newfound knowledge about the impact alcoholism had on families. One quote from Father Joseph Martin in one of his videos was "Never be impressed with people who hold degrees; after all rectal thermometers have them and you know where they put them!"

In the early 80s, after taking courses in an alcohol and chemical dependency studies program at a local college, she was introduced to the early, middle, and late signs of the disease of alcoholism. This was the first time with all her education she not only realized what a stereotype she had of an alcoholic, but also recognized how angry she was at the educational system because it had not taught her about the one subject that had affected her life more than anything else. Around this same time she also began driving clients from a local rehab to another twelve-step program, where she heard others' stories. At first she compared herself, but slowly she started to identify when she heard them speak about their own experiences.

She was a slow learner. After four and a half years of attending meetings to learn how to help others with their alcohol problem, she experienced a wake-up call. She realized she had a problem with alcohol and needed help.

Thus, her knowledge does not come from reading tons of books or paying thousands of dollars for classes; it comes primarily from being an active listener in a multitude of meetings in four different self-help programs, and attending conferences, retreats, and workshops in a wide variety of places. She heard people share honestly of their pain, denial, experiences, strength, and hope. These experiences are the foundation of her journey that could have given her a PhD in the study of alcoholism. She became a student in the "University of Life".

Recognizing her own alcoholism was a major turning point in her life. Not only did it have a major impact on her personal life, but it also enhanced her abilities as a teacher. She touched some of her students' lives in a way she never could have imagined. She could now recognize the "overachiever", "scapegoat", "lost child", and "mascot" in her classrooms. She incorporated some of her lessons around subject matter relating to alcohol or alcoholism. For example, she had sixth graders write about the three stages of alcoholism. Becki gained some of the children's trust so those who were living in a home with the three ground rules- do not ask, do not talk, and do not feel - could express themselves and reveal their feelings.

THIS JOURNEY HAS SPANNED OVER three decades, during which she attended numerous conferences and workshops. Some of the most significant were ACCEPT '81 (Atlantic City Conference on Education & Prevention Techniques). ACCEPT '83, and Annual Conferences on Alcoholism and the Family 1982–1986. In 1986, the conference changed its name to the Annual Conference on Chemical Dependency and the Family because the coordinators realized it didn't matter the substance or the behavior; the dynamics affecting the families living with any addiction were basically the same. In 1985, she went to California to attend TRIBES, a program which taught people how to work cooperatively in groups. She was the only person east of the Ohio River to be qualified as a trainer of trainers. In 1986, she attended the National Youth to Youth Conference in Ohio and the Family Restoration Workshop with Sharon Wegscheider-Cruise. In 1987, she went to the Third Annual Conference for Adult Children of Alcoholics. She was selected as an adult staff member for the Annual Youth to Youth Conferences in 1987–1989, where she quickly became known as "the warm fuzzy lady," and in August 1988, she was part of the First Annual Western Youth to Youth Conference in California. In November 1989 she participated in the Codependency and Intimate Relationship Conference in Florida.

In the early '90s, Becki and another coworker planned a Superintendent's Day on alcohol awareness. She remains active and the following article adds a little more to her accomplishments and illustrates how helping others allows her to pass on what she has been so freely given.

VOLUNTEER

(Reprint of 1999 article)
Taken from the Hamilton Hall Herald, a newsletter
of St. Lawrence Alcoholism Treatment Center
December Issue 5

Variety is the spice of life, says an old adage. Until recently I did not realize the extent of volunteer work I had done throughout my life.

Once upon a time I began my volunteering in a nursing home during high school. It has continued to the present day in various ways. While my two daughters were young, I taught Sunday school. Eventually I became Superintendent of Sunday Schools.

Late in the 1970s, I became a volunteer at the St. Lawrence Alcoholism Treatment Center. I drove patients to outside 12-step meetings, made a rotating schedule coordinating seven other volunteers, and got a dozen or more new recruits so more meetings were available to the clients.

Understanding more and more about addiction from attending numerous national conferences, workshops, retreats, I began a community prevention program called AIM AHEAD (An Involvement of Many—Awareness and Helping in the Education of Alcohol and other Drugs). Another important accomplishment was writing a weekly column in the At Your Leisure section of the local Sunday paper for over five years. The articles were all related to addiction and ran about five years.

Next, I began to share this information using another format. I made presentations and did trainings. One presentation was Expanding Our Horizons in Prevention at the 1986 NYFAC (New York Federation of Alcoholism Counselors) Conference. I also trained the local treatment center staff on Communication and Listening Skills for STAFF (Strategies and Techniques Affecting a Facility's Fellowship).

Then I served on different committees and boards. St Lawrence County is the largest county in New York State and the only one without a council. Serving on the original committee to establish a council for alcoholism, I was elected in 1986 to be on the first Board of Directors of The Alcohol and Substance Abuse Council of St. Lawrence County and then honored to be its president for two years. In addition I was asked to serve on the board of the North Country Freedom Homes, the Advisory Committee to the Mater Dei College Alcohol and Chemical Dependency Program, and also on the Community Advisory Board at the local treatment center.

Energetic, eager, earnest, teens kept me young at heart from 1985–1996 while working with Youth to Youth and YES (Youth Educating Society). A weekend every month or so found me, aka "The Warm Fuzzy Lady" at a Youth to Youth conference in a high school somewhere in New York State. The highlight was going to Russia and Ireland with a group of 50 teens and staff for a couple weeks in 1992 and with another similar group to Australia in 1995.

Every Thursday night from 1992–1999, I taught a recovery workshop at the local treatment center. "I have found GOD" (Good Orderly Direction), "I am not NUTS" (Not Using The Steps), and "I use TOOLS" (Techniques Offering Options with Love and Support) were just a few of the topics shared. Another project undertaken at this local treatment center was to gather recovery materials for the facility's library.

Recognized with awards such as volunteer of the year at the treatment center for 1994 and 1995 was a great honor. Then in 1999 I was awarded the volunteer of the year for the Northern Tier Providers Association of Alcohol and Substance Abuse Services. (Given to an individual who has given of their time and talent to provide assistance to the client community, promote community treatment and/or prevention efforts or advocate on behalf of those in need.)

YEARS AGO, I WAS PROMISED that I was "going to go places, meet people, and do things I never dreamed possible." A couple years after that it was promised that I was "going to go places, meet people and do things I never dreamed possible **beyond my wildest dreams**." These volunteer experiences played a big part in fulfilling those promises.

Notes

Notes

Notes

www.ingramcontent.com/pod-product-compliance
Lightning Source LLC
Chambersburg PA
CBHW031330290526
45784CB00014B/2464